MAN THE F*CK UP

How To Pick Yourself Up And Succeed
When Life Bitch Slaps You

MARK LLEWHELLIN

Book 6 in the
Mark Llewhellin
Success and Happiness Series

DEDICATION

This book is dedicated to the love of my life, my little miracle, Léon James Llewhellin, who I love more than anyone in the world. You are kind, thoughtful, well balanced and you are already achieving great things in your life.

You are my biggest reason for having my life in order, and staying strong in challenging times.

Words cannot describe how much I love you and how proud I am of the person you are.

This book is also dedicated to those of you who are going through challenging times.

GET TWO OF MARK'S BOOKS FOR FREE

Join Mark's team for information on new books along with special offers and pick up a FREE copy of Mark's 5 star reviewed books:

'The Underdog' and 'Delusions Of Grandeur.'

Details can be found at the end of this book.

TABLE OF CONTENTS

INTRODUCTION 1

EMPOWERING STORIES 9

WHEN YOU THINK YOU CAN'T GO ON 17

YOUR REASONS TO MAN UP 31

HOPE THROUGH HORROR 43

WALKING ON FIRE 65

HAVE A WORD WITH YOURSELF 71

CLEVER THINKING 81

ASK FOR HELP 97

CHUCK AWAY YOUR WEAK ASS THINKING 107

NO EXCUSES 115

STOP BITCHING, MAKE THAT CHANGE, AND GO FOR IT! 125

ACKNOWLEDGEMENTS 137

ABOUT THE AUTHOR   138

ALSO BY MARK LLEWHELLIN   141

MARK LLEWHELLIN BOOKS OUT IN 2020   144

GET TWO FREE MARK LLEWHELLIN BOOKS   145

INTRODUCTION

"I am not what has happened to me.
I am what I choose to become."
– Carl Jung

Man The F*ck Up

One evening in September 1974, nine months after I was born, my Dad Ken sensed that something wasn't right.

My Mum had been suffering from depression and had locked herself in the bathroom.

Unaware of what was unfolding behind the bathroom door, my Dad started shouting, "Pat, Pat, are you ok in there?"

My Mum didn't respond.

Fearing the worst, my Dad lifted his leg and kicked the door as hard as he could. The door flew open and to my Dad's horror, he could see a husband's worst nightmare unfolding right before his very eyes.

My Mum was holding a pair of scissors in her hands, had blood pouring from her chest, and was fighting for breath.

She had stabbed herself in the chest with the scissors!

My Dad knew that he was racing against the clock. There was no time to phone an ambulance and wait for help to come. It would take the ambulance at least twice as long to get my Mum to the hospital, so my Dad put my Mum straight into his car and drove to the local hospital.

He knew if he was to save her life, time was of the essence!

When they arrived at the hospital, the staff did everything they could and the good news was, the stab wound wasn't going to end her life. However, there was a much bigger problem! My Mum had taken an overdose of prescription drugs and when the doctors asked her what type of drugs she'd taken, she refused to tell them.

I was only a baby at that time and was oblivious to what was going on. However, what happened over the course of those next few days would change my life forever!

The doctors fought to save my mother's life and after two days in critical condition, the doctor told my Mum's parents and my Dad the worst news any parent and husband could hear.

"We're sorry, but there's nothing that we could do."

My Mum had flatlined and despite the doctor's best efforts, she was gone!

She was a kind, gentle, loving person, and was liked by everyone who knew her. The devastating news hit like a tsunami wave going over my entire family.

My Grandad, Sid, and my Nan, Angela, had lost their beautiful little girl. My Dad had lost his wife. My Aunt Diana had lost her little sister. And me and my older brother Darren had lost our Mum.

She was only 26 years old.

By the time I was 9 months old, my Mum had killed herself, my Dad decided he didn't want to raise me, and my future looked uncertain and bleak. Some things that happen in your life will be brilliant and you'll treasure every moment. However, some of the things that will happen to you will be as welcome as a turd in a swimming pool!

The reality of life is, it doesn't matter how strong you are, at some point:

Life will shock you!

Life will upset you!

Life will reduce you to tears!

Life will bring you to your knees!

And life, my friend, will you rip you apart and spit you out!

Make no mistake about it, life will be brutal at times, and there will be nothing that you can do to change the unpleasant situations that have happened to you.

Sooner or later, life is going to deal you a massive shit sandwich, and you're going to have to eat it… whether you like it or not!

No matter how tough you are, or how tough you think you are; one day, life will come knocking on your door, and it will come into your home and bitch slap the fuck out of you! You'll desperately try to avoid it, but it will follow you out of your home and bitch slap your ass, in your car, in the shops, and in your friend's and relatives house.

And life will continue to bitch slap and kick your weedy little ass up and down the street until you're at the point when you've had enough and you feel you can't take any more!

If you've lived long enough, then you've probably already been through it. It's happened to me, and it's happened to, or will happen to, every human being I've ever known.

This book won't be able to change challenging situations that have happened to you. However, it will help you to control your mind and get you through the challenges that you're facing. Life is a mind game, and how you play that mind game will determine whether you win or lose in life!

When you read the title of this book, you may be expecting some sort of hard-nosed, not giving a fuck type of person to tell you to 'man the fuck up' and get on with things. There is an element of truth in that, but there are certain circumstances where it's not quite as easy as saying, "Man the fuck up and get on with things."

Yes, there are times when we need to say to ourselves and our friends to "just get on with it." However, when a devastating bit of news has been given to someone, it certainly isn't the right time. In a case such as the loss of a loved one, we obviously need to support people in a gentle, more loving manner.

What I'm hoping that you'll takeaway from this is some inspiration and hope.

In this book, I've written about people who faced

horrendous challenges but decided, for one reason or another, to get a grip and make the most of their lives. The people that I've written about in this book, didn't just 'man up' and get on with their own life, they also helped and inspired other people.

I'll also tell you about the techniques that I have used to get through some of my own challenges in the hope that it will help you in some small way.

Rather than just read this book like it's any other book, read it as if your life depends on the information in here, because one day, it just might!

CHAPTER 1

EMPOWERING STORIES

"You may have spent your whole life talking about yourself in a negative way, but that doesn't mean you have to continue that path. The way you choose to think and speak about yourself is a choice."

– Miya Yamanouchi

One day I asked my Dad if he had any video footage of my Mum. I'm not exactly sure how old I was, but I'm pretty sure that I was somewhere in my 30s.

I've seen lots of pictures of my Mum but I had never seen her moving, walking, smiling or breathing. At least not that I remember, as I was only a baby when she died.

My Dad told me that he had some cine film footage from the 1970s of him and my Mum. I asked if I could have them and went to work on finding a company that could transfer the cine film onto a DVD. Sure enough, I found a company, and in the post several weeks later, I had in my possession DVD footage of my Mum.

My Dad told me that the footage was the trip they went on to Venice, Florence, Nice and a few other Italian places. It also had footage of my Grandad Sid, my Nan Angela, me and my brother Darren.

I sat down with my Dad in a small bedroom in his house and put the DVD player on. I honestly didn't think that watching it would have any effect on me whatsoever. Why would it? My Mum died when I was a baby, and besides, I had already seen loads of photos of her. So it was no big deal, right?

Wrong!

As the DVD played, my Mum came on the screen. She was laughing, she was smiling, she was full of life, and then, it hit me like a sledgehammer!

I started to lose control of my emotions! But how could this be?

I'm as tough as they come (at least that's what I tell myself). No moving images on a screen are going to rock me, in any way shape or form.

But this cine film footage of my Mum was my kryptonite!

Regardless of me always thinking how super tough I am mentally; I felt a wave of emotion building up in me, and then, something unusual started to happen... my eyeballs started to sweat!

At least that's how I like to explain it. I'm a grown man

and I don't cry. But all jokes aside, it deeply affected me. The tears built up and then, they slowly ran down my cheeks. There was no sound in the footage but it was so impactful seeing my Mum smiling, walking, breathing and enjoying herself. At the same time, it was also heartbreaking!

I hadn't cried in front of my Dad since I was about eight years old. That was when my brother Darren, AKA the most evil child since Damien off 'The Omen' movies; chased me onto a beach and wrapped a tennis racket as hard as he could around my legs.

He was a right little bastard!

Smashing bricks on people's heads, shooting me with an air rifle, and smashing doors down to get at his little brother. It was all in a day's work for Darren when he was younger. Fortunately, as he got older, he chilled out massively, and is now one of the nicest people that I know.

Of course physical pain is a lot different to emotional pain and when most people get older, they are less likely to cry from physical pain. But emotional pain can still reduce the toughest of the tough to tears, no matter what age they are.

I couldn't even put my finger on it. Why did this bring

tears to my eyes? I mean, I didn't even really know her, did I?

I sat next to my Dad on the bed watching the footage and as the tears came, I covered my eyes with my right hand and wiped them away. My Dad sat next to me and nodded. He had a look of sadness on his face, and I knew that it also affected him deeply.

After the DVD had finished, I stood up slowly, said goodbye to my Dad, and walked out of his house in a zombie like daze.

Watching the footage affected me because it was so personal and also because I could see how happy she was at that time. It was so tragic that she died so young and under such horrible circumstances.

But the death of my Mum has never affected me before I watched the DVD, or since I watched the DVD.

I was talking to a friend one day who said that her partner's father had killed himself. Her partner was also only a baby when his Dad killed himself, but it negatively affected him throughout his adult life.

We'd both gone through similar things, but it's never had a negative impact on me. So why does it affect him a lot more than me?

It all boils down to the story we tell ourselves.

I was told that my Mum had postnatal depression. In the 1970s, postnatal depression wasn't recognised like it is now, and there is a lot more help for people suffering with this. I could've blamed myself for her death, but I never have and I never will. How could I? I was only a baby at the time.

When somebody takes their life, it isn't the fault of anybody else. Nobody forces someone to take their life. The choice is down to the individual and the individual alone!

When you blame others for how you feel and how you think, you're playing the role of the victim, and that is a weakness you must overcome.

You're better and stronger than that and you can overcome whatever has happened in your past by the story you tell yourself.

So make sure you tell yourself stories about yourself that empower you!

CHAPTER 2

WHEN YOU THINK YOU CAN'T GO ON

"It is not in the stars to hold our destiny, but in ourselves."
– William Shakespeare

"I don't want to be here anymore!"

These are the words I said to myself in the year 2002. I was in a situation I perceived to be hopeless. I had left the army three years earlier, was now in my late 20s and living back with my parents. So much for the success I planned for myself.

I was trying to set up a running event that was going nowhere fast. I was in debt £43,000 from my spending sprees in my early 20s, which were from bank loans and running up credit card bills to the max. And I also owed a local T-shirt company £1,600.

Ironically, the £43,000 debt didn't bother me much because I was in debt to banks that have billions of pounds. I knew they weren't going to struggle because I hadn't paid off a £4,000 or £6,000 loan.

But I didn't like owing a local business money because I

knew that they weren't flush with cash. I just wanted things to be easier. The crazy thing about all of this was, it was a time in my life where I hadn't gone through my biggest challenges.

Heck, it wasn't even close to the worst circumstances. Those are left to losing loved ones and I've been through that. You can convince yourself that things are much worse than they are. Even though you may feel hopeless, there is always hope and you can always make it through to the other side!

It was just a time when I wanted my life to be easier. You've probably had the same thing in your own life where you've had a guts full, and you want to live a happier, less complicated life.

It's possible to become so focused on what is going wrong, that it can be very difficult to see the positives in your life. And when I was very down and at the lowest point of my life, I wasn't thinking about anyone else apart from myself.

You may not want to be here. If that's the case, then I know how you feel because I've been in a similar situation where I no longer wanted to be part of this planet.

Life, or life as I interpreted it, wasn't going my way. I was fed up with suffering, I was fed up with the despair that I was feeling, and I wished all the pain could just go away.

I was never at the stage where I had planned my death out. You know, what type of rope do I need?

What type of tape is the best one to to seal a hosepipe on your exhaust?

"Sellotape? No, not strong enough."

"Gorilla tape? Fuck yes... Gorilla tape will do the job!"

What sort of pills should I take? Make sure it's not the blue ones because an overdose with them would have different effects on your body.

I remember talking to one of my mates and he said that he took a Viagra pill once and felt that it wasn't working. So after 20 minutes he took another one. I asked him how that rolled for him. His face became very serious looking, and he said, "It was a fucking nightmare!"

Still laughing, I replied, "What, what happened?"

He told me that after taking the second Viagra, he was rock hard!

"So what's the problem?" I said.

He told me he was hard for a solid (no pun intended) 24 hours!

At this point I was in hysterical laughter, but he still had a very serious look on his face. I was now on a roll and said, "Did you put your speedos on and go to the swimming pool?"

Not impressed with my childish remarks, he said it became very painful and he was almost at the point of going to the doctors.

This sent me into further hysterics!

That story still puts a smile on my face but all jokes aside, I remember not wanting to be a part of this planet anymore. And if you focus on what's wrong and you're always thinking about yourself, it can be difficult to break out of that.

When I thought I didn't want to be here anymore, I had gone into a very dark place in my mind. It's difficult to explain to somebody that hasn't felt that low. One thing is for sure though. You stop being grateful for your life.

Your sole focus is to think about the problem you've either

got or something unpleasant that has happened in the past.

With suicides, it wasn't just my Mum that killed herself in the family.

My Grandad Percy also took his life. Why? I still don't know to this day, but all I know was he went down to some woods and strung himself up on a tree. His own Son, my uncle Michael found him.

I've never spoken to Michael about it, but my Dad said that Michael was shouting when he found his Dad. When my Dad heard Michael shouting, he started running towards the woods to get to him. But before he got there, one local, who had already seen my Grandad Percy, got to my Dad before he could see his father hanging there.

"Don't go in there!" He told my Dad and stopped him from seeing what Micheal had just seen.

There was also my Dad's cousin Peter, who also hung himself in a barn. He left behind his heartbroken parents Ralph and Ray, his wife Anne and his young son Matthew.

Going further back in my history, there were more of my family members who also came to a tragic end.

When I was at my lowest point I can remember standing in the bedroom in my Mum's house and thinking to myself, "Fuck I'm cursed! Cursed with the Llewhellin tradition of killing ourselves!"

So what brought me out of the darkness?

At the point of my deepest despair, I remembered what my Dad said to me in the past,

"What many people don't understand is, when they take their lives, it doesn't take away their problems. They have to deal with their problems in the next level. Killing yourself makes things worse. Worse, because your spirit lives on and you can feel the pain that you've put your loved ones through."

"WORSE, WORSE, HOW CAN THINGS BE ANY WORSE?!" I remember thinking to myself.

I thought, "Fuck, I can't even kill myself and get out of the shit I'm in!"

Everyone has their own belief on whether there is life after death. Some people believe that there isn't, but how do we 100% know that there's not? We don't!

So there is a possibility that taking your own life will lead to making things worse than they already are if you're in a dark place. Regardless of what has happened to you or your family in the past, that doesn't mean it has to be your future. If you go back far enough in your family history, there will be relatives that have lived a happy, healthy and successful life.

If you want to get out of the hole you're in now, or if you ever find yourself in a deep dark hole in the future, my thoughts are with you. I want to tell you I really care about you as a person, even if we don't know each other or have never met.

I don't enjoy seeing anybody suffering, and one of my biggest joys in life is seeing other people happy and enjoying their lives.

So the next phrase I'm going to say to you may seem like I don't care about you. It may also seem like I'm just throwing something out there, but I want you to know that I am with you, and do care about you. As do many other people even if you don't think they do.

"You're going to need to man the fuck up and take charge of your life!"

If you follow the principles in this book, there is a fantastic future out there waiting for you. And you don't want to miss out on it.

The year of writing these words is 2020 and I have to say that my life now is awesome. But what if I would have taken things a step further and ended it all in 2002? I would have missed out on so many great things that have happened since, I would also miss out on the days I have after writing these words.

Most importantly, my amazing Son Léon wouldn't exist if I hadn't focused my thoughts on solutions to my challenges.

Maybe there was a time in your life that was your darkest time. Think back to a time in your life that was very dark. If your life would have ended what cool things would you have missed out on that you later experienced?

Make a list here:

1 ....

2 ....

3 ....

4 ....

5 ....

6 ....

7 ....

8 ....

9 ....

10 ....

11 ....

12 ....

13 ....

14 ....

15 ....

16 ....

17 ....

18 ....

19 ....

20 ....

The chances are, there's a lot of things you still want to do with your life. So think about, or even better, write 20 things that you would like to do or have in your life.

1 ....

2 ....

3 ....

4 ....

5 ....

6 ....

7 ....

8 ....

9 ....

10 ....

11 ....

12 ....

13 ....

14 ....

15 ....

16 ....

17 ....

18 ....

19 ....

20 ....

No matter what has happened in your past or no matter how you're feeling now; if you make changes, you can live the life that you always dreamed about!

CHAPTER 3

YOUR REASONS TO MAN UP

"It is during the darkest moments that we must focus to see the light."
– Aristotle

What is your reason to pull through when times are tough?

Mine is a 10-year-old little boy who needs his Daddy to be strong. But even before Léon was born, I couldn't just give up on life when things were hard, and neither should you!

If your life is about YOU YOU YOU and you decide not to care about others or you decide not to help people, your life will be infinitely harder than it needs to be. However, if you care about others and you help people with their challenges, life will be more fulfilling and you will live a much happier, more meaningful life.

If you have a big enough reason to pull yourself up out of a dark place, then you'll do it. One of the biggest reasons for getting through your most challenging times is because there is a fantastic life out there waiting for you!

You might already have an amazing life compared to millions, if not billions of people around the world. So look around and think about what you can feel grateful for in your life. If you don't have to walk many miles to a well to get water, then you're already ahead of millions of people around the world.

If you're a parent, then just being a role model to your child should be a good enough reason, and if it isn't, why isn't it? Are you focusing on what's best for your child, or are you focusing on what's more important for you?

One day I was dropping my Son off to his Mum, and as I looked in the rearview mirror, I could see that he was in tears.

"Léon what's the matter?" I said.

"My belly really hurts daddy."

For a parent, there's nothing worse than seeing your child in pain.

As I stopped the car to wait for his Mum at the meeting point, I asked Léon to climb into the front seat with me so I could give him a cuddle. I knew it was important that he needed to feel loved.

I said to him what most parents think when they see their child in pain, "If I could take away your pain and put it in Daddy's belly, I would, but unfortunately I can't do that." If you're a loving parent, you'll probably think the same thing and you would gladly take on your child's pain if you could take that pain away from your child.

Taking a child's pain away physically is just as important as taking away their mental and emotional pain. As parents, we have to be mindful of what is going to hurt our child emotionally and avoid that any way we can.

If you're moping around feeling sorry for yourself all day long and telling everybody how hard your life is, that's of no benefit to you or any other person. Sure, if we're going through a challenging time, then it can be an important to share our troubles. But if we've been complaining about life for the last few months, or the last few years, then it's time to get a grip of ourselves and get our shit together!

Some people who think about taking their own life think it's better if they're not around, and that it will be better for the people who they care about.

That's a cop out!

If you want to put your loved ones through a severe amount of pain, killing yourself could do the job. If you take your own life, then that will have a massive negative effect on the people that love you the most!

Love it or hate it, when you are going through tough times, the most important thing that you can do is man the fuck up, and take positive steps to sort your life out! You are the one that needs to set an example, and you are the one that needs to be the hero in your loved one's life.

I was walking down a street one day listening to a podcast that had best-selling authors Steve Scott and Barrie Davenport on it. The podcast episode was about getting into the writing habit. As I was walking with my head down, I glanced up to my left and saw a car with a big silver badge on the back saying 'LEON' which is a model from SEAT, a Spanish car company owned by the Volkswagen Group.

I immediately thought that was just what I needed to see.

We all interpret things differently and sometimes we can dismiss signs right in front of us, which is natural. But this time, something struck a chord in me and told me, this is why I need to form a new writing habit, I need to do it for my Son Léon.

Like all parents who adore their children, I want to do the most I can for my Son and have experiences with him that will stay with us forever. This is also one of the major reasons for writing this book.

Manning up and getting a grip isn't just about when you're going through a challenging time, it can also be when you need to take action to make things happen so you can create a better future for yourself and the people that are closest to you.

Maybe you don't have children, but even if you don't, there will still be someone that loves you or someone that you can inspire. If you're having a pity party most days, then you need to get your shit together!

You are a winner and you'll become more of a winner when you set a good example and help others!

Hero characters in movies aren't lazy bastards who sit on their hands and do nothing for themselves or for others. They are the people who have taken on very tough challenges, backed it up with massive action, persistence and don't give up.

If you had a choice of what character to be in a movie, which character would you be? It's obvious you would want to be the hero or heroine.

Think about it. If you're an actor and the director or

producer offered you a part, would you just want to be one of the extras? Of course not. You'd rather be the leading lady or the leading man.

You want to be the star, you want to be the hero, you want to be the person that kicks ass and wins the day!

Imagine a chat between the director and actor.

Director: "I'm making a big budget ass kicking movie, and I want you to be in it."

Actor: "Cool, what role would you like me to play?"

Director: "Well, you have 2 choices."

A: "You can be the badass hero of the movie."

Or

B: "You can be the person who is weak and gets wasted halfway through the movie."

Actor: "I want to be the badass hero of the movie!"

Director: "Are you sure? I don't mind if you take the part of the weak character that gets wasted."

Actor: "No thanks, I want to be the hero."

You want to be the James Bond, the John Rambo, the Rocky, you want to be the girl out of the Hunger Games or some other female hero!

Children have people they would like to be like, and if you're a parent, your child needs to have someone that is mentally strong and can support them in their own challenging times.

I don't think I'm alone, but I'd rather be the hero in my Son's eyes than someone else. Of course there are people on TV he'll admire. In Léon's case (at the time of writing) it's Olympic and Marathon champions.

If you want a better life for yourself and your loved ones, you need to:

- Man up for your family.

- Man up and help your friends.

- Man up and inspire people you have yet to meet.

- And most importantly, man the fuck up and help yourself!

A depressed woman who is financially successful spoke to personal development coach Tony Robbins and told him how bad things were going for her. Tony asked the woman if she would like to be free.

She replied, "Free of what?"

Tony said, "Free of depression."

The woman told Tony how much she loved her daughter and he replied, "If you loved your daughter you wouldn't be beating yourself up like you're doing, because it's not helping her, is it?"

He's 100% right!

You may look like you've got your shit together on the outside, but on the inside, if you're always hurting, then you can't call your life for a success. However, you can change that!

You need to look after yourself, because if you don't look after yourself, you won't be very effective with helping other people. Whether that's your family, your friends, or somebody you have just met.

So when times are tough, remember your reasons to man the fuck up.

No matter what challenge comes your way...

You are strong enough to overcome it!

Man The F*ck Up

CHAPTER 4

HOPE THROUGH HORROR

"I wish none of this happened," said Frodo.
Gandalf replied,
"So do all who live to see such times. But that is not for them to decide. All we have to decide is what to do with the time that is given to us."
– J. R. R. Tolkien (The Lord of the Rings)

Man The F*ck Up

Immaculée Ilibagiza lived a beautiful childhood.

The weather was glorious, her neighbours were friendly, she loved her family dearly and was deeply loved by her parents and her three brothers. She lived in a developing country and the children in her area walked on average eight miles from their homes to and from school. Their parents were never worried that anything bad would happen to the children because the neighbourhood was safe and friendly.

Immaculée's Mother was a religious woman and prayed a lot for the health and wellbeing of her family. Her parents also taught Immaculée and her brothers to treat her friends and her neighbours with respect. Sometimes, Immaculée's family would let people stay with them if their friends had fallen on hard times and they were struggling to survive.

Her parents were very well respected in the community

and always tried to help people as much as they could.

When Immaculée was 10 years old, she moved to a new school. This was a new experience for her and it was exciting times, but those exciting times turned into unpleasantness when she was asked by the teacher what ethnic group she belonged to.

Her teacher asked her if she was Tutsi or Hutu?

Young Immaculée sat in her chair totally bewildered and had no idea what the teacher was talking about. She wasn't aware of the different ethnic classes and because of this her teacher got very upset and threw her out of class, which brought her to tears. Even though she was very well educated from her parents, they didn't want her to find out about the divide of ethnic groups because her parents were the type of people who treated everybody the same.

It wouldn't matter to them what ethnic group they were from, and they believed that everybody was equal. The reason they didn't teach her about the different ethnic groups was because they didn't want her and her brothers to feel different to other children.

When Immaculée moved up to the next school at the age of 15, she excelled in her education and came second out of a class of 60. She planned that one day she would eventually go to university and was excited about the possibilities and her future.

Her parents told her that if she had enough determination and worked hard, she could become an important person in the community one day.

She wanted to take her education to the next level, but even though she was one of the very top students, she still didn't get a scholarship and was passed over for a Hutu child that wasn't as good as her academically. This news was deeply upsetting to the entire family. When she told her Father the news, he closed his eyes for what she described as the longest time. Shortly after without saying another word, he went to his room. To say he felt upset would be an understatement.

That evening Immaculée cried her little heart out!

She worked hard to get the grades she got, and she believed that by achieving her high grades it would lead to a scholarship; so she could get a better education, but it was out of her hands. In her society, the family knew that without the higher education, Immaculée would have no prospects, no rights, and no respect in the community. She was only 15 years old, and because she was passed over for a scholarship, she now believed that there would be little hope for her to live the life that she dreamed of living.

The next morning, Immaculée's Father woke up and sold their two family cows to help Immaculée get a better education. Many people in their community simply didn't have the money to own two cows. It was not considered a good financial move selling one cow, let alone two because it could lead to extremely hard financial times for the family! However, as far as her Dad was concerned, he was willing to give everything that he could give, whether it was a lot of money (which he didn't have), or his two cows.

Selling cows meant that he could pay for a better type of education for his daughter. It wasn't the scholarship to the top school that she wanted, but at least it was something, and it would definitely brighten her prospects for the future. The school that Immaculée ended up going to was a right 'shit hole' by Western standards.

The walls were rough, they didn't have any paint on them, and she ended up sleeping next to 10 other girls all crammed together in a small room. With no running water at the school, the children would have to walk two miles to the nearest stream to get the water that they needed.

However, her family knew, she would have a better

chance at that school than if she had no school to go to. All Immaculée and her family could do was make the best of the situation! Immaculée didn't let this deter her and she chose maths and physics which were the hardest courses she could take; and again, she worked extremely hard and became one of the top students.

Her brothers teased her and said that her place was in the kitchen which she didn't find funny.

Whenever somebody would try to put her down, even though it was only teasing, it simply gave her more determination, and she went out into the world with an 'I'll show you attitude!'

Her dream was to go to a better school, but in her heart, she believed that she wouldn't get into one because she was a Tutsi. Despite this, she still put her best effort in. To Immaculée's delight, regardless of her ethnic background, she was accepted into one of the best schools in her country. Unfortunately, at the same time, fighting broke out between Hutu and Tutsi groups in certain parts of the country.

This was a very frightening time, and when Immaculée went outside of her school grounds, she sometimes had threats from Hutu men in the area. With all of this going on, she started to give up on her dreams of going to university and had severe doubts about where her future would take her. However, she kept on working extremely hard and as if by some miracle, she got a scholarship into one of the best universities in her country!

The family celebrated and were ecstatic, especially as she was the first girl in her family to qualify for university. Immaculée was delighted, and when she arrived at her university, she was enjoying every minute of it.

Her scholarship also qualified her to receive $30 a month. That doesn't sound much to people in the Western world, but to her it was a lot of money. In her third year of university, hatred was spreading more and more amongst the ethnic groups. The Hutu leaders wanted to attack the Tutsis and told the Hutu people that Tutsis would attack them at some point, so the Hutu people might as well attack first.

When Immaculée returned home to spend time with her family on her university holidays, her brother alerted the family there were Hutu men that had a list of Tutsi people in the area and they were going to kill them. Of course this put a lot of fear into the family, but Immaculée's Father tried to calm the situation down and told him that he was overreacting.

Their Father had heard stories before of death squads that

were supposed to come around and kill them, but it never happened. He reassured the family that this wasn't going to happen and there was no need for them to flee their home and cross the border into a different country.

Of course this was deeply disturbing to the family, but they believed Immaculée's Father, took his advice, and decided to stay put. Later that evening, they prayed as they usually did and went to bed.

Early the next morning, Immaculée's bedroom door flew open, and she was awoken by a frightened brother who told her that the President of their country had been in his plane when it was shot down. The man that they believed was going to bring peace to the country had been killed!

The Hutu leadership had promised that if the President was killed, then all of the Tutsi's in the country would be executed! That same morning, Immaculée and her family had heard on the radio that Hutu's had started killing Tutsi's in the night and they found out that the Hutu killers had killed her uncle!

It was at that moment they realised that they should've got out of the country the night before as Immaculée's brother had wanted. Shortly after they had heard the news about their uncle, there was an announcement on the radio that told everybody to stay in their homes and the only people allowed travel were military personnel.

That day they stayed in their home and listened to the radio and heard that Hutu civilians had joined government military personnel and were killing innocent Tutsi families. It wasn't just the innocent and unarmed men that they were killing; they also killed women, children, and babies!

The local radio stations then encouraged Immaculée's neighbours to pick up machetes and kill Immaculée, her Mum, her Dad, her Brothers, and anyone else that was a Tutsi. That morning, while at home, they could hear screams from the village below.

They walked outside of their home, which was situated at the top of the hill only to see an innocent neighbour being surrounded by Hutu men and hacked to death with machetes!

Immaculée and her family soon learned that they were completely surrounded, and escape was now virtually impossible. They had left it too late to escape and now all they could do was hope and pray!

Immaculée's Father told her that she had to leave their home because he believed that she would be safer with their local pastor. The pastor was a Hutu, but they believed he was a good man and believed that he would help protect people. She reluctantly left them and went to the pastor's house to hide but she also bumped into Hutu people that she knew on her way to find a hiding place.

Immaculée was delighted when she saw her old schoolteacher, but she was shocked to see that he now looked at her like she was scum, and had no time for her! She was heartbroken because this was a man that she knew and felt that she could rely on, but through no fault of her own, things had changed!

Shortly after that, she was delighted to see her best friend from her school days and knew that her best friend would welcome her with open arms. However, it wasn't to be.

Her best friend was a Hutu and now became completely cold to Immaculée and wanted nothing to do with her!

Thankfully, the pastor was friendly and when they were out of sight from any Hutu, he hid her in his bathroom, which was next to his bedroom. She had visited the pastor's house many times before, but for one reason or another, she had never noticed the bathroom attached to his bedroom.

Immaculée hoped that if she had never noticed the bathroom with all of her visits, then maybe the killers wouldn't notice it either if they ever came into the house.

She wasn't alone in the bathroom and found herself with a 14-year-old girl, a very frightened looking 12-year-old girl, who was still wearing her school uniform, a 55-year-old woman, the woman's daughter who was a similar age to Immaculée, and a 7-year old little girl.

The room was so small that they ended up lying on top of each other with the smaller children on top of them so everyone could fit in. It was extremely hard to sleep because of what was going on, and also because of the other people that were moving around next to her.

She would also wake up in the night with cramps because she was relatively static for such a long time in the cramped little bathroom.

Immaculée and her new friends were given very little food from the pastor and were starting to lose weight. They knew if they kept on getting only tiny bits of food (that came from scraps from the pastor's family), they would suffer from malnutrition.

The reason the pastor couldn't give them much food was because if he started shopping for more people than he normally did, the locals would notice it, search his house, and kill the women and the little girls!

They couldn't talk to each other for fear of being heard by their neighbours (who had now turned into their hunter/killers) and developed their own form of basic sign language to try to communicate with each other.

They could hear chants outside the house and Immaculée peered outside the bathroom window, she could see hundreds of people gathered and chanting "Kill them all!"

Some of the people wielding machetes that joined the murderous group were once friends of Immaculée and her family, and they had even been over to Immaculée's house to have dinner with her and her family.

Outside of the pastor's house there were horrendous things going on.

Babies had been taken from their parents and had been hacked to death with machetes in front of their Mothers and Fathers and then the Mum's and Dad's would be hacked to death!

Immaculée's (once friendly) neighbours would also rape families, chop their limbs off (sometimes including their heads), and put the dead bodies into huge piles. When they weren't in piles, the dead bodies of Immaculée's Tutsi neighbours were left in the street where starving dogs ate them!

One night, Immaculée heard a Mother being killed and the Mother's baby was left out in the street to either die from heatstroke, lack of water, or be eaten by wild animals.

Immaculée's neighbours were going from house-to-house, searching high and low, and when they would find people hiding; they would either slaughter them then and there, or they would bring the poor victims out into the street and publicly slaughter them!

One day, there were hundreds of people outside the pastor's house, they were chanting,

"Kill them, kill them, kill them all, kill them big, kill them small!"

The killers then pushed their way into the pastor's house. Immaculée felt despair and fear like never before as she could hear the killers move from room to room looking for her and her friends. She believed her death was only seconds away!

As if by some miracle, they never came into the pastor's bedroom or the bathroom that Immaculée's and her friends were hiding in. After they had left, the pastor told them that the killers will be back soon, of course this was harrowing news from Immaculée and her friends.

Immaculée noticed that there was a wardrobe in the pastor's bedroom, and she asked the pastor to slide it across because it was just big enough to block the bathroom door. However, the pastor refused and said that the killers would look behind the wardrobe, see the door and be even angrier.

Immaculée believed that if the killers saw the door (with no wardrobe in front of it), the killers would walk straight in next time and that would be the end of her and her friends!

She pleaded with the pastor to move the wardrobe in front of the door, but he still refused. Immaculée couldn't believe what she was hearing and got on her knees and begged the pastor,

"Please I'm begging you, I know in my heart if you don't put the wardrobe in front of the door, they're going to find us the next time they search. Don't worry if they get angry, they can only kill us once!"

Reluctantly, the pastor agreed and slid a wardrobe in front of the bathroom door. Shortly after, the killers came back to search his house again.

In her book, 'Left To Tell' Immaculée said,

"I heard the killers call my name, they were on the other side of the wall. Less than an inch of plaster and wood separated us. The voices were cold, hard, and determined.

"She's here, we know she's here somewhere. Find her. Find Immaculée!" Said one of the killers.

Immaculée said,

"There were many voices, and many killers, I could see them in my mind. They were former friends and neighbours who once greeted me with kindness. Now they were going through the house, calling my name while carrying spears and machetes."

"I've killed 399 cockroaches" said one of the killers, "Immaculée will make 400, it's a good number to kill!"

Immaculée said,

"I cowered in the corner; I held my breath so the killers wouldn't hear my breathing. Their voices clawed my flesh, I felt that I was lying on a bed of burning coals. I never realised that fear could cause so much agonising pain!"

Immaculée wondered what it would feel like when the machete slashed into her skin and cut into her bones. She wondered if her parents and brothers were still alive and thought that if they're not, she may soon be joining them in heaven.

She held onto her Fathers rosary beads and asked God to spare her life. The killers went but came back sporadically over the next three months.

In the past, churches were always a safe haven for people in Rwanda and even though killings had happened before the 1994 genocide, churches were off-limits for killing, but this time it was different!

There were reports of large amounts of people hiding in the churches, which were burnt down with innocent men, women, and children inside!

When some people tried to flee to escape the fumes and the flames, they were immediately slaughtered by the blood-thirsty killers with machetes, spears, and knives that waited for them outside the church.

During the massacres, Immaculée felt hatred towards people and wanted nothing more than to kill all of the Hutu's.

Immaculée's normal weight was a very slim 115 pounds but while hiding in the bathroom, she lost another 40 pounds – turning her to skin and bone. Her lips were cracked, she felt incredibly weak and because she hadn't washed, showered, or changed her clothes, body lice attacked Immaculée and all her friends!

They were also getting ill.

Normally they could go to the doctors and get a pill which would clear things up within a day or two. But now they had nothing, and they just suffered with whatever illness, pain, or disease they had!

Immaculée had no way of knowing if she would ever get out of that cramped bathroom but she started to believe that it was possible and asked the pastor if he could give her some books on English, so she could learn the English language.

She had dreams of working with the United Nations and knew that to get such a job, she would have to speak English. She hoped that one day, the United Nations would come in and rescue her.

One of the pastor's Hutu cleaners asked if he could clean the bathroom, but the pastor refused and told him to leave. The cleaner grew suspicious, and the pastor feared that his own cleaner was about to tell the Hutu killers to look into the bathroom.

Time had run out for both the pastor and all of the women and children hiding in the bathroom. If they were found in the bathroom, not only would they be killed but the pastor would also be killed for hiding them!

The pastor let them out the next morning and they headed to a (temporary) United Nations French camp, which had recently been set up to protect Tutsi men, women, and children from being killed.

If they made it to the camp, they knew that the French soldiers would protect them. Immaculée and her friends made it to the French camp and eventually, after another close encounter with death, made it to safety.

When she got out of the bathroom after 91 days, she found out that all of her material possessions had either been destroyed or stolen. Her neighbour's had been killed, her school friends had been killed, two of her three Brothers had been killed, her Dad had been killed, and her Mum had been killed!

It is estimated that up to one million people in Rwanda were slaughtered in the space of only three months!

After the genocide was over, the Tutsi's that had been driven away into different countries came back into Rwanda and Hutu killers were held accountable for their crimes and jailed.

Immaculée ended up going into a prison to face the person responsible for the death of some of her family. He was brought into a room and Immaculée soon realised that it was her Father's friend! She even remembered playing with his children.

He was a successful businessman but turned into a killer and hoped he would get all of Immaculée's family's possessions and land.

There is obviously only so much of Immaculée's story that I can put in this book, but I can highly recommend that you get her book: 'Left To Tell' to find out more of the details.

Here are some of the things that we can take from this story:

- The head of the family, organisation, religion, community, or country isn't always right.

- Put your best effort in, even if the odds are against you.

- Having a brilliant start in life doesn't mean it's going to be plain sailing throughout your life.

- Life isn't always fair.

- Some people who you trust can turn on you.

- Just because you're a good person it doesn't mean that life won't hurt you.

- Even if you're nice to certain people, they may not be nice back.

- Visualise the outcome that you want.

- There are people out there in worse situations than you.

To say that life was tough for Immaculée would be a complete understatement.

Many people wouldn't blame Immaculée for living with bitterness and hatred in her heart, feeling sorry for herself for the rest of her life and becoming a mental wreck of a person. However, Immaculée decided that she was going to make the best of her life despite the horrific circumstances that she had been through at an early age.

Amazingly, she forgave the people that caused her so much suffering, moved to the United States, became a New York Times Bestselling Author, a World Class

Motivational Speaker and is the recipient of the Mahatma Gandhi Reconciliation and Peace Award.

When I listen to Immaculée's audiobook, I am humbled and blown away by this incredible woman that had turned her life around after such horrific experiences.

So if Immaculée can turn her life around and turn tragedy, loss, and suffering into triumph, so can you!

CHAPTER 5

WALKING ON FIRE

"I've had a lot of worries in my life, most of which never happened."
– Mark Twain

Sometimes we'll feel like a little hedgehog crossing the road. There is a great opportunity at the other side, but we might get squished along the way. Many people think they can't do a certain thing because they think they can't.

In 2017, my friend said he was going to go to a Tony Robbins event. I had listened to Tony Robbins on YouTube and found a lot of his information helpful.

I told my friend I'd love to go to one of those events one day to see what it's all about. It turned out that my friend was tied up on the date and being the good egg that he is, he gave me and my friend two free tickets.

The opportunity was too good to miss, I listen to a lot of Tony's YouTube videos in the past, so I didn't think I would learn a great deal more. Although I always think to myself, you can always learn new things, and things can always be refreshed.

But one of the major reasons, and the biggest draw for me, was there was a fire walk in the event. I had wanted to do a fire walk for the last 20 years, but never got around to doing one. Now this opportunity had appeared and there was no way I was going to miss it.

Many people may think to themselves, you're a crazy motherfucker for wanting to do something like that. But I knew, or at least I thought I knew, this was all down to your mindset.

It turns out that most people who do a fire walk don't get burnt. But it's still a hell of a thing to walk over the hot coals with a heat of 1000°F.

Several days into the event, the moment I had been waiting for came. We all took our shoes and socks off and walked out of London's O2 arena towards the hot coals outside. One by one people walked across the hot coals because they had got their minds into a mental state where they believed they could do it. They believed not only that they could walk across the hot coals; they believed that they wouldn't get burnt, and as far as I'm aware nobody got burnt.

Does this mean you're some super person? Not really.

And let's be honest, there's only so far that you can walk

on hot coals before they burn the living fuck out of your feet! I mean, if the fire walk was 2 miles or a marathon long. The chances are, you'd be lit up like a Christmas tree!

What was interesting about the fire walk was it signified that:

Many of our fears are only in our mind.

And

We can get through to the other side, when we put our minds to it!

Yes, if you tried to walk on fire for a whole marathon, you would perform some sort of self cremation service. So there's always going to be limitations to what a human being can do. But we never know what we can do until we push the boundaries!

This was a fire walk on a hotbed of coals for only a few feet. But whether or not we like it, we're all going to do the fire walk of life!

Sometimes we will have tremendous fear, sometimes we will get burnt, and sometimes we will breeze through things and they will be easier than what we thought they would first be. I know some people who make themselves out to be fearless, but all of us have fears.

When I was a boy, I believed that a commando or a bodyguard was somebody that never gets frightened. But when you become these things, you realise it isn't true. The perception of these two types of people is more of an exaggerated Hollywood version than what it is in actual life.

We all have fears, but if you have a big goal and you feel that by reaching that goal your life will be better, then you need to be bold and go for it!

And if I can achieve the things I've achieved from where I've come from; then there is no reason you can't also achieve great things with your life.

So man the fuck up and go for it!

CHAPTER 6

HAVE A WORD WITH YOURSELF

"All that we are is the result of what we have thought.
The mind is everything. What we think, we become."
– Buddha

Man The F*ck Up

In the army, if you said or did something stupid, often the response that would come back to you would be, "Have a word with yourself." Which when translated means: you're talking a load of bollocks so think about what you are saying before you say it.

In life you need to take control of your thoughts, because if you don't carefully think about what you're thinking, your life can spiral out of control in a terrible way.

Ultimately, there is no one path to getting through tough challenges.

There are millions of people with a religion that have struggled. And there are millions of people without a religion that have also struggled. On the other side of the coin, there are both religious people and non-religious people who do equally well in life.

So how is this possible?

If you believe that there is a source that is giving you strength, whether it's God, or you just believe in yourself, all of those things can be just as effective as the other.

If you believe that God is giving you strength then you will get strength from that. If you believe that you were destined to be a strong person and you don't believe in God, you will also get strength from that. If you have gone through more challenges than the average person, it gives you an opportunity to help people that are facing challenges themselves.

I can remember when I was in the army we were travelling on the bus one time and someone called me ugly. This really upset me.

At the time I had had little experience with girls, and it wasn't until I was 18 that I slept with a girl. That wasn't anything to do with my looks, it was my confidence, because I felt scared to death to ask a girl out because I feared rejection.

I knew that I was getting left behind in this department so I had to man the fuck up and be willing to face rejection. The alternative to this would be to live a life where there were fewer girls in my life. Of course, when you're in your late teens or early 20s, forming relationships is a huge part of your life.

At that age, you don't want to be left behind because not only do you feel you're missing out, but you also know that your mates will take the piss out of you. Most guys like to feel special and being at the bottom of the pile is not very high on their agenda and it's that way with girls · too.

On 5th November 2018 I was visiting my Mum. While there, I saw a news broadcast on the TV about a man that had taken his life which they said was down to PTSD and all the things that he had seen in conflicts abroad.

His wife came on the telly and she mentioned that he was not in a good state mentally because the people trying to help him, continually asked him what had happened.

She said that this process made him worse because he kept on reliving the situation all the time. She mentioned what he needed to do was get his mind off thinking about it all the time and not being reminded about it.

If you're always looking at the past, and thinking about the horrible things that have happened in your life and you're struggling mentally, you need to look towards the future!

People can argue all day about the different psychological techniques and which technique is the most effective for helping people. Ultimately, there is no one cure for everything. All that matters is what gets you the results you want so you can live a happier and healthier life.

Regardless of what techniques people use, it always comes down to what you say to yourself.

Tell yourself negative things and you will get negative results!

But if you tell yourself positive things, you'll get positive results!

Some people will bitch about what I just wrote and say things like, "Well you don't understand my situation, it's unique, and that will never work." These people give up before they're even willing to put a massive effort into something. And if you don't have an open mind and put the effort in, then you've already lost!

My Mum/Aunt Diana who brought me up knows a thing or two about going through hard times.

She had a miscarriage.

Then she had a still-born baby boy.

She then lost another child called Sandra that was only

one week old.

After that, her sister (my Mum) killed herself.

Her Mum Angela died.

She went bankrupt.

Her Dad Sid died.

She's been suffering with arthritis for many years.

She's had cancer.

And her husband Des died.

When I asked her how she handled all of this, she simply says, "You've got to handle it, you've got to look forward."

Most of us have negative memories.

It could be losing a loved one, losing a friend, falling out with someone, being told that you have lost your job, getting accused of something you didn't do, going bankrupt or having a relationship go pear shaped.

If we keep on re-living the negative thoughts we have, we

can never move forward.

Maybe this therapy will work with some individuals. Maybe they feel better about talking about all the trauma they went through. There's nothing wrong with that if they feel it's helping them, but when it becomes a problem, is when it makes them worse.

Many of us can feel relieved when we talk about what's happened to us, but many people will just relive the nightmare in their own mind, and it will make them worse.

There is no simple solution to this as we are all unique and we have to treat the person individually rather than have some blanket method which is to talk about your traumatic time or not to talk about your traumatic time.

Either way,

"Your past does not determine your future. Your thinking in the present moment will determine your future!"

This is so important that I'm going to repeat it again. In fact, it's so important that I'm going to highlight it in big bold ass letters and give it its own page...

"Your past does not determine your future. Your thinking in the present moment will determine your future!"

Man The F*ck Up

CHAPTER 7

CLEVER THINKING

"Although the world is full of suffering, it is also full of overcoming it."
– Helen Keller

In 1942, 300 years after the death of the Italian astronomer, physicist and engineer Galileo Galilei, a baby boy was born in Oxford, England.

And just like Galileo, this baby boy's life would follow a similar path. As he grew up into a young boy, he loved to know how things worked and spent a lot of his time alone with little interaction with other boys.

In school he studied intensely, and his classmates called him Einstein. This was something which appealed to his ego and also encouraged him to be even more knowledgeable. Not that he thought he was Einstein. But he knew he was very smart and would go on to achieve great things.

His parents expected him to go to Oxford University and thought it was a great idea if he studied medicine. However, he didn't want to study medicine, and eventually, came to an agreement with his father that he would do a degree in natural sciences and specialise in physics.

Back then, many of the professors at Oxford thought that you were brilliant or not brilliant. And if you weren't as intelligent as the children that picked things up straight away, then you just had to accept your place. However, this young boy didn't like to accept his place, and he didn't like people telling him what he was and wasn't capable of.

During his last year at Oxford he noticed that his balance was becoming an issue and falling over was becoming a regular occurrence. At first he thought it would be something trivial, and ignored it, but then one day, he fell down the stairs, knocking himself unconscious and giving himself temporary amnesia!

He soon recovered, and even though he didn't put much effort into his undergraduate studies, he still graduated with a first class honours degree; he then moved on to Cambridge University to begin his PhD. At this point in his life he had no idea what was going to happen, either professionally or personally. He believed that things would get better.

However, life can be unpredictable and can throw a curveball your way. I wouldn't call it a curve ball that was thrown to this young man. It was more of a medicine ball fired from a rocket launcher!

After arriving at Cambridge his balance issue became more pronounced and soon after he made an appointment to see a family doctor. However, he was quickly referred to a medical specialist in London. The specialist admitted the young student into hospital for tests, and he was diagnosed with motor neurone disease (MND).

Motor neurone disease is a progressive neurological disorder that destroys the cells in the spinal cord and the brain that controls muscle activity. It affects breathing, walking, swallowing, moving and a whole load of other things that most of us take for granted. With motor neurone disease, the muscles waste away and the ability to control muscle movement is gradually lost.

This motor neurone disease bombshell made him realise that he took things for granted. Walking from one room to another, or picking up a knife and fork to eat, would soon, through no fault of his own, become impossible! If this wasn't bad enough news, he would shortly be told that he only had 2 to 3 years to live!

This was a devastating blow not only to himself but also to his parents, the rest of his family and all the people that loved him. To say this news took the wind out of his sails was an understatement!

One thing that had a positive influence in his life was a fellow student who he had fallen in love with. She made him realise that there was a point to carrying on his research and life was not over!

When we look more into this, he knew that he was going to lose his physical ability, and he must have thought that she might want to be with another man. However, he continued with his studies, which brought new battles of an academic nature.

He would speak about his progressive theories with some brilliant, older, more experienced, respected scholars, and they blatantly didn't agree with him. Some people believed, not only had he lost his ability to move freely, but he had also lost his ability to think logically.

The young man relentlessly carried on in his pursuit of the truth, or at least the truth as he saw it. He eventually won his peers over with his ground-breaking research on cosmology, which started a wave of academic credibility that would ripple across the globe!

This young student also looked on the positive side of life, and knew that despite the challenges with his body, his brain wasn't affected.

Because he didn't have much time to live, he decided to double his efforts, to answer some of the biggest questions in cosmology.

Example:

- Did the universe have a beginning or not?

- What is the nature of time?

- Will time ever end?

- Can we go back in time?

- Who are we?

- Why are we here?

A lot of scientists didn't like the Big Bang theory, because it pointed towards one specific point in time where there was a moment of creation. In other words, did God create everything in one enormous boom? However, the gifted cosmologist asked a different question. He asked if there could be a Big Bang without God?

He believed the key to such a question could be unlocked with black holes! His thesis, despite being controversial, boosted his global reputation.

As well as having motor neurone disease and trying to understand the mysteries of the universe, he had two (and later three) children with his wife Jane. Although feeling delighted with having his two children, his physical body was failing fast!

He didn't want to ask for outside help, so he relied heavily on Jane for tasks like getting washed and dressed, etc.

When he gave his first lecture about the subject of black holes, a professor jumped to his feet in disgust, and said, "This is utter nonsense!" It was hugely controversial. But most of the scientific community eventually accepted his theory. It was known as 'Hawking radiation.'

That young man is none other than Professor Stephen William Hawking!

From that point on, many opportunities came Stephen's way, and many openings materialised.

In 1974, The California Institute of Technology (Caltech) offered him a visiting professorship which he accepted as he believed sunny California may stimulate some new thinking! He wanted to write a book about how he believed the universe had begun and dreamed about it being sold in shops and airports around the world as a massive bestseller!

He got a literary agent called Al Zuckerman, who later said he didn't think it would work because there are no other books like Stephen's in airports.

Stephen completed the first draft of the book and was pleased with how it went, but Peter Guzzardi (Stephen's book editor from Bantam Books) was disappointed with it, and thought it would be extremely hard to create a good book out of the draft that Stephen gave him.

However, that was the least of Stephen's worries, as he got a chest infection that turned into pneumonia, which became life threatening! Stephen was put into a drug-induced coma and put on a life-support machine. Things were very bleak, and it got to a point where the doctors thought there was no way he could ever come back.

They asked his wife Jane if they could turn off the machine and let him pass away but she refused!

Amazingly, Stephen survived, but when he woke up his medical condition had got much worse and he had lost his ability to speak, as the doctors had to perform a tracheotomy (which involved cutting a hole in his neck and placing a tube into his windpipe so he could breathe).

It was hard for him to be optimistic, and he began to believe that his book would never be released, and his life was pretty much over. He would later describe these days as the darkest of his life!

With writing his book, it was painstakingly slow and at this point Stephen could only communicate by raising his eyebrow when somebody showed him a letter so he could make up a word. Sometimes I thought that I wasn't producing enough words for my books, but I guess this puts everything into perspective.

If you're working on something where you need to produce words, you may struggle to produce the 500, 1000, or 3000 + words a day. But you can only imagine the incredibly slow pace Stephen was working at with somebody having to point to a letter for him to make up a word.

Regardless of his pace, he was persistent, and then one day, a glimmer of hope came from across the pond in the United States. A team of people had created a system called 'Equaliser,' where a computer screen contained rows of letters at the top and at the bottom of the screen there were rows of regularly occurring words. This completely changed how fast he could write his book!

Even though his pace was slower than a normal able-bodied person, in several months, Stephen had rewritten the book.

The publishers took a gamble whether anyone would like it, but like it people did!

It became the number-one best-selling book in the world and it stayed on the bestsellers list for four-years, which earned it a place in the Guinness Book of World Records!

Although it was an incredible success, it wasn't without casualties. The fame and fortune put such a strain on both Stephen and his wife Jane that they were no longer happy in their marriage, and the marriage fell apart and it ended in divorce.

An interesting thing that I found when conducting research on Stephen Hawking was that one of the happiest times of his life was when he was younger and first in love with Jane. It wasn't when he had the fame and money.

Stephen married his second wife Elaine, who was at first one of his carers, but she also said that the strain of fame took its toll on their marriage; and when the press started looking into their private lives, that marriage also eventually ended in divorce.

One of the most challenging times Stephen went through at that point was when the press said there was domestic violence, which was very hurtful for both Stephen and his wife. The police later dropped the inquiry into the assaults, but the mental damage took its toll. However, they spent 11-years of their life together and many of those times were happy memories.

Stephen communicated with a switch on his cheek and also used a facial recognition system, where a high-speed camera took pictures of minute facial expressions, which improved Stephen's speech with his famous robotic voice.

In his own words he said,

"I have lived over two thirds of my life with the threat of death hanging over me. Because every new day could be my last, I have developed a desire to make the most of each and every minute."

In the same year I was born – 1974, Stephen was inducted into the Royal Society, which is one of the scientific community's most prestigious bodies. He is a recipient of the Presidential Medal of Freedom, which is the highest civilian award in the United States.

In 2002, Stephen Hawking was ranked as one of the hundred greatest Britons; he came in at number 25. Like

Sir Isaac Newton and Charles Darwin, Hawking achieved great things, and he is at the time of writing without question the most famous scientist since Albert Einstein.

Even into his 70s he kept working at Cambridge University and believed that keeping an active mind, along with keeping a good sense of humour was the most important thing that kept him alive for so much longer that his doctors had first predicted.

On the 14th of March 2018, aged 76, Stephen Hawking passed away.

Even though the doctors predicted in his early 20s that he didn't have much time left, he lived and achieved great things over the next 50 years!

When Stephen Hawking was first diagnosed, he could have sat in the corner and cried every day for the next few years until the end, but he didn't.

He manned the fuck up and made something of his life!

And if he can man the fuck up and achieve great things with all the challenges he had; then you and I have no excuses to not go out there and live the incredible lives that we are destined to live!

Here are some things that we can learn from Stephen's life:

- If you're going through a difficult time, find reasons to live.

- Be grateful for what you've got.

- Adapt when life knocks you down.

- Have goals.

- People that should support you may doubt you.

- Take on big challenges.

- Keep moving towards your goals, no matter how slow things are going.

- Look for possibilities.

- Question things.

- Just because something doesn't normally happen, it doesn't mean it can never happen.

- Contribute to people's lives.

- Get an excellent team of people around you.

- Be an inspiration to people.

- Keep going when life looks grim.

- Always try to maintain a good sense of humour.

"However difficult life may seem, don't give up."
– Stephen Hawking

CHAPTER 8

ASK FOR HELP

"Be strong enough to stand alone. Smart enough to know when you need help. And brave enough to ask for it."
– Mark Amend

Man The F*ck Up

We all need help in life.

Man the fuck up doesn't mean that you should stay quiet and suffer in silence if you are going through a difficult time. It means you need to be brave enough, and strong enough, to know when you need support and ask people to help you.

In fact, even if you're not going through a troublesome time, you're still going to need help from other people.

If you've ever seen the Oscars, then you'll know that when somebody wins an award, they always mention the people that helped them.

When an actor wins an Oscar, even though they may be the star of the movie; there is no way that they could've got that Academy Award without the help of the:

- Director

- Producer
- Executive producers
- Special effects team
- Stunt men and women
- Unit production managers
- Casting people
- Costume designers
- Composer
- Orchestra
- Singers
- Song writers
- Bodyguards (for the A-listers)
- Make up team
- Visual effects supervisors
- Animation supervisors
- Associate producers
- Assistant directors
- Conceptual designers
- Supervising sound editors
- Sound designers and re-recording mixers
- Music editor
- Postproduction supervisors
- Doubles
- Project consultants
- Camera operators
- Runners
- Language translators
- Set production assistance

- And the author, if the film was adapted from a book.

But even without the people that they work the closest with, there are many people that helped them achieve their goal.

These will be the pilot and the airline staff that took them to the locations to film. It will be the drivers that got them from A to B. It will be mechanics, electricians, engineers, plumbers, builders, carpenters and other skilled trades people that helped.

With the Lord of the Rings trilogy, they had a production team of over 2,400 people, and had 26,000 extras that worked on the films for five years. Peter Jackson was the man responsible for directing, co-producing and co-writing the screenplay for J.R.R. Tolkien's incredible novels 'The Lord of the Rings.'

But he couldn't have made the films, let alone won as many awards as he did without the help of thousands of people. There are many times when I am striving towards a goal and I know that I need help off other people.

An example of this is I'm not very good on computers, so I ask friends to help me with that kind of thing. By asking people who are better than me in certain areas, it helps reduce my stress levels because I can struggle with these things. It's one reason why it's very rare that I get stressed. I know if I don't enjoy doing something, there are people out there that are far more efficient than I am that can help me. So I ask them to help.

We can't do everything ourselves, and there are people that are just better than we are at doing certain things. So if we can get them to help us, it will make things a lot easier for us.

Many people will enjoy helping you as long as you give them credit for what they've done for you; or if you can help them in some way. Whether it's by paying them or opening doors for them. Some people need nothing, they just like helping you.

Even at the time of writing this, I know a lady who wants to get her first book published. I know that she can give me little in return. She doesn't have many contacts, she doesn't have much money, in fact there is nothing that I want from her.

I just like helping her because I enjoy it and I want to see her achieve her dream of publishing a book.

There will also be times when you're going through tough challenges and you need help from others. If you feel that life is dragging you down too much, never be afraid to ask for help from somebody.

In America, it's a fairly popular thing to have a therapist, but not so popular in the UK. In the UK, having a therapist is a lot more stigmatised, whereas it's not such a big deal in the United States.

You may not want or feel you need to go to a therapist. But if you go down that route, make sure you know that the therapist has got their own life together. That person needs to have an impressive track record with helping people, and they need to be mentally strong. Having a PhD in psychology or psychotherapy doesn't mean jack shit if they haven't got their own life in order.

I've never needed one myself, but that's not to say that somebody else shouldn't use one. Most paid professionals don't just do it for the money; most of them genuinely want to help people live a happier and more successful life.

My mental strength and high confidence level mainly comes from reading books on personal development, and it's one of the reasons that I now write books on this very subject. I know that if I can turn my life around, then so can others by learning the things that I have learnt.

An author of personal development and psychology

books can help you massively, but if you want to talk to somebody personally, an author can't always be there for you.

When you need someone to talk to, you need to find somebody that you can trust and someone you know that you can confide in. If that person has gone through a lot of challenging times, they can be more understanding of your situation. And they help you get through it by telling you how they got through their challenges.

Ideally, you need to talk to someone that also doesn't blab to everybody else about your problems.

Women are generally better than men with sharing problems and talking things through.

Ultimately you need to:

- Admit there is a problem.

- Ask for and accept help.

- Believe it's possible for things to get better.

Many people don't want to ask for help because they think:

- The other person will laugh at them.

- The person will criticise them.

- The person won't want to help them.

There are many people that will want to help you if you're going through a hard time.

Most people feel good about helping someone else. Think about a time when you've come to the rescue of someone in need. If you're a half decent person you would have felt that you did some good with helping someone, and it probably made you feel good too.

If someone comes to you with a problem and asks for help, it means that they respect you and they respect your opinion over a lot of other people's opinions.

Most people like to give an opinion and like their opinion to be valued, so ask them if you feel you can trust them and they can help you.

One of the comedy series that I used to enjoy watching was the American TV show 'Scrubs.'

The show follows several unique and interesting characters in a hospital. At the start of each show there is a short theme tune, and it says the words...

"I can't do this all on my own, I'm no Superman...I'm no Superman!"

Obviously Superman is a fictional character, but even the toughest people in the world need help.

So if you're struggling, then man the fuck up and ask for help!

CHAPTER 9

CHUCK AWAY YOUR WEAK ASS THINKING

"If you always put a limit on everything you do, physical or anything else, it will spread into your work and into your life. There are no limits. They're only plateaus, and you must not stay there, you must go beyond them."
– Bruce Lee

On the 10th of March 1940, a baby boy by the name of Carlos was born in Oklahoma. When Carlos was a child, he described himself as non-athletic, shy and mediocre. His father drank a lot of alcohol and went on heavy alcoholic binges, which lasted for several months at a time.

When he left home, Carlos joined the United States Air Force as a policeman and was based in South Korea. In Korea, Carlos took a keen interest in martial arts which he continued when he returned to The United States and was based in California.

When Carlos left the U.S. Air Force, he applied to be a police officer, but at the same time he opened up his own martial arts studio.

Even though he had achieved nothing as a child, he was a very driven person as an adult. Carlos found that the more effort he put into something, the more he would be rewarded financially and the more recognition he would get.

He started entering martial arts competitions and things didn't always go his way, but he would learn from his losses.

Carlos put lots of hours into practising his craft and ended up winning a national championship and many other big championships. This gave him more credibility and opened more doors for him.

He started training celebrity clients. One client was Steve McQueen, who suggested that he should take acting seriously. He also became friends with Bruce Lee, and Bruce also encouraged Carlos to take up acting more seriously.

This gave Carlos more confidence and this confidence, along with his celebrity contacts, helped him get a foot into the movie industry.

Carlos not only became an actor but also a film producer and a screenwriter.

He said,

"A lot of times people look at the negative side of what

they feel they can't do. I always look on the positive side of what I can do."

Carlos became an author and wrote books about martial arts, exercise, philosophy, politics, religion, fiction and his own biography.

He became a New York Times bestselling author and starred in films such as 'Lone Wolf McQuade,' 'Missing in Action,' 'The Delta Force,' Bruce Lee's 'The Way of the Dragon' and Sylvester Stallone's 'The Expendables.'

Carlos' full name is Carlos Ray Norris but we all know him as Chuck Norris.

After his books and his fame in the movie industry, he gained even more fame as his 'Chuck Norris Facts' became an Internet meme. These Memes document funny, fictional, and absurd feats of strength and endurance.

Here are some of them:

- When Chuck Norris does push ups, he doesn't push himself up, he pushes the earth down.

- Chuck Norris can kill a stone with two birds.

- A king cobra bit Chuck Norris. After five days of

excruciating pain, the cobra died.

- When Chuck Norris swims the ocean, the sharks are in a steel cage.

- Superman once challenged Chuck Norris to a fight. The loser had to wear his underpants on the outside.

- Chuck Norris split the atom with his bare hands.

- Chuck Norris plays soccer with a bowling ball.

- When Google has a question, they 'Norris it.'

- Chuck Norris can hear sign language.

- Chuck Norris can bake a cake in the freezer.

- When the bogeyman goes to bed at night, he checks the closet for Chuck Norris.

- Chuck Norris can moonwalk forwards.

- Chuck Norris counted to infinity... twice!

- Chuck Norris ordered a Big Mac from a Burger King and got it.

- Chuck Norris can understand women.

Chuck Norris overcame his non-athletic abilities and shyness as a child and didn't let the challenges with his father affect the rest of his life in a negative way.

He manned the fuck up and went on to achieve incredible things with his life.

He did this by:

- Having a dream.

- Visualising what he wanted.

- Taking lots of action towards his dreams.

- Getting around the right people who could help and support him.

- Being nice to other people.

- Telling himself that he is a winner.

- And he 'manned the fuck up' during the toughest times in his life!

Man The F*ck Up

CHAPTER 10

NO EXCUSES

"Beast mode doesn't make excuses. It doesn't complain. Whatever you're doing, go out there and get it done. Keep pushing."

– Matt Kemp

One of the major reasons people fail to achieve the things they want, is because they always find an excuse not to do the things that need to be done to achieve their goals. An outstanding example of this is Emma, who was one of my personal fitness training clients.

Emma said she didn't want to go outside training because the weather was horrible. I explained to her that there has been a new invention called the waterproof jacket she could get. Emma burst out laughing and immediately understood what I was talking about.

Some people think you need to have a lot of money to be in great shape. Which is them basically pointing out they're not in shape because they aren't a celebrity who can afford personal trainers and nutritious food.

Now and again I hear somebody saying, "Oh, it's okay for that celebrity, they've got a personal trainer and they've got the money to stay in shape." The reality is, rice doesn't cost much money, pasta doesn't cost much money, potatoes cost little money and, tuna doesn't cost much money. Healthy eating doesn't cost much money.

Being in great shape is nothing to do with how much money you have, but it's got everything to do with your mental state.

If you want to find an excuse then you will, but if you want to improve your life, you have to set goals and you have to be committed. There's always a way to achieve your goal, especially if millions of people are already achieving what you want to achieve.

One evening I was talking to a friend and the subject of her going to the gym came up.

She harped on about going to the gym and 'getting into it,' but she was avoiding it. And she had put on more weight than she was happy with. Since I had come into her life, she had slowly lost weight and was feeling better about herself.

When looking for an excuse, she said, "You aren't me and don't know what it's like to have lived with anxiety all your life."

To which I replied, "Are you telling me for the past 30

years of your life, you haven't been able to find any solutions from books or other people to help you with this challenge?" All I got from her was silence. It was as if I could hear the cogs turning around in her head. My question made her think.

If she answered, "No, I haven't been able to find anything that could help me in the past 30 years of my life," it would make her look like a dumbass.

If you want to find out the answer to the question you have, the chances are you're going to find the answer to that question. It's easier than ever to find answers to your challenges today. All you have to do is type your question into Google or YouTube, and there's a good chance the answer is somewhere there.

Have you taken every action you can to reach your goal? And if the answer is no, then you know you need to take more action!

When you are constantly doing everything there is that can be done to improve your mental health, fitness or whatever else it is; you'll get results!

By constantly doing – I mean that you've been doing it day in day out for a good 6 months! This is where many people screw up. They tell themselves (and other people) they've tried. Tried often means dabbled.

They may have read one or two personal development books and done some exercise two or three times a week for 3 months and not felt better or seen much improvement. If that's how often you're exercising and you're not getting the results you want, then it's time to get serious and put more effort into it!

Be 100% honest and ask yourself, have you done every little thing that you can do to improve your mental health?

Do you:

- Exercise?

- Get yourself around kind and encouraging people?

- Read and study lots of personal development books?

I'm only human and I can get knocked down and hurt with situations. However, the reason I don't get hurt as easily and I recover far quicker than the average person is because I continue to work on my mental attitude day in day out.

If you want to get fantastic results in your life with being happy and achieving your goals, you can't just try to do the right steps then give up. Personal development has to be an ongoing thing every single day!

Picking up one book and saying that you've read that book and tried the principles in it but it didn't work, is like saying that you had a bath twice in your life but it never kept me clean throughout all of my life.

If you want to stay clean, then you need to have a bath or a shower every day and it's exactly the same with personal development. If you want to achieve your goals in life, then you have to work on your mind every single day!

You may find it a challenge at the start, but the more you do it the more likely you are to form a habit and then it will just become a part of your day.

Most people don't do this, they just drift from day to day not putting much time into their personal development, and if a challenge comes up, they moan about it and try to scrape through it themselves.

As the saying goes, "No man is an island."

We all need other people to help us. Whether that's indirectly from a book like this one, and watching an inspirational movie, or listening to a song that lifts you up, we all need an outside source to help us.

Sometimes I've heard stories about these mystic people that sit in a cave for 30 years and somehow they get all the answers in life. However, they've experienced very little in life. How many countries have they been to? How many people have they interacted with?

In other words, you're not going to get much wisdom by sitting in a cave, being a lazy bastard and doing fuck all!

Personally, I want to be out in the world helping other people and not sitting in a cave for 30 years, or even a year would bore the living shit out of me! But hey, different things for different people.

Just before my book 'The Underdog' was published, my former girlfriend said something great.

"Your book is brilliant when it's being read, but when someone finishes it, they can just go back to their normal negative thinking."

She had a good point.

Lots of people get inspired by something briefly and then forget about it as soon as the next day begins, or as soon as a challenge comes their way. So how do we store our new, better way of thinking into our internal system?

We do it by making it a habit, we do it by continually educating our minds and feeding our minds with things that will help us overcome challenges.

My friend Wayne Martin said to me that in all his life, he'd never met anyone like me. He'd never met anyone who has the same level of optimism and happiness. It was a kind compliment, but there isn't anything I've done that most other people couldn't do.

The only thing I will take a little credit for is I've been careful with the people I hang around with, and I've made sure that I've fed my mind with positive, inspirational things every day.

No matter how positive or tough you are, there will be times when you fall down and get hurt. However, when you take action every day towards building a stronger mindset, you will recover far quicker!

So take action every day that will strengthen you!

By doing this, you will become a much happier and more confident person.

CHAPTER 11

STOP BITCHING, MAKE THAT CHANGE, AND GO FOR IT!

"If you can't fly then run, if you can't run then walk, if you can't walk then crawl, but whatever you do you have to keep moving forward."
– Martin Luther King, Jr.

Man The F*ck Up

Have you ever come across someone who moans and groans and wants to let you know how hard things are for them?

In 2016, I was listening to someone who was making a right meal of letting me know how hard things are for him. He was up in years, but throughout most of his life he's always been one of these people who wants you to feel sorry for him.

Most of us have our down times or times when we feel as if life is giving us one hell of a beating. However, when there is nothing wrong with you or you've got very little to complain about it, don't moan!

This person just wanted me to feel sorry for him and wanted attention.

When I came across the quote from Stephen Hawking, I knew it had to go into this book.

I look at some challenges I've been through in life and think about some of the times when I've felt sorry for myself; I thought about how Stephen Hawking would react if I was standing in front of him and told him something like:

I've lost my job

Or

I've lost my house

Or

I'm tens of thousands of pounds in debt

Or

My relationship didn't work out

Or

I haven't got much money left, etc.

If you get up most mornings whingeing, or you blame other people because your life hasn't turned out like a Disney fairytale, then you are literally the universe's little bitch!

This isn't what the complainers in life want to hear. They don't want to take responsibility for the way their life has turned out. However, if you want to create a better life for yourself, then you need to realise that YOU are the one that is responsible for the actions you take next!

Those actions, if formed into good habits, will lead you to a much better place in life!

Stop complaining about little things.

Many people spend a lot of their lives complaining about silly little things, and because they focus their attention on small things going wrong, they make themselves unhappy.

One morning, I woke up and needed to go for a pee. There was only one problem with this situation, I felt warm, I felt comfortable, and I'd only just woken up, so I was still a little sleepy. I'm sure you've been in the same situation.

You're in bed, you need to go to the toilet, but you can't, or should I say, 'you won't!'

Eventually you get out of bed, you go to the loo, you relieve yourself and you came back into your nice cosy bed. But how long did you lie in your bed before you got up to go to the toilet?

Sometimes I have laid in bed for 5, 10, 15 or even 20 minutes in discomfort when I could've got rid of the discomfort and got back into my nice, warm cosy bed without the pain in my bladder.

This happens with people in life too, and it often happens with things like jobs and relationships. Some people are 'kind of' happy where they are in a job or relationship, but not thrilled or fulfilled.

The big question is, "How long you do want to keep the pain going for." Some people will stay in relationships years longer than they should do and waste their lives away.

Some people stay in abusive relationships. Sometimes it's not just the men that are doing the abusing (whether it's physical or mental), it can also be the women that are dishing out the verbal or physical abuse.

Many people stay with their partner because they feel afraid of what the partner might do to them, or they feel afraid of being alone.

These situations can be challenging for people, and I know it's easy to say "man the fuck up," but if you're unhappy with your life and want to make a change then guess what, 'It's time to man the fuck up and make that change!'

If I didn't make myself clear, I will subtly say it again...

It's time to man the fuck up and make that change!

If you decide you want to stay with that person and keep on bullshitting yourself by saying things like, "It might get better," after years of abuse. To put it bluntly, you've just fucked up your life!

I know somebody that is constantly complaining about her job. Every day she would go home from work and tell her partner that work is very stressful, and she was glad the day was over.

She was one of these people that just couldn't wait for the weekend to come.

She started applying for new jobs, and after a lot of persisting a new job opportunity came up and the company offered her £13,000 more than she was earning. All she had to do was drive an extra 15 minutes to work.

It was a dream situation for her, or at least you'd think it was a dream situation for her. But even though she was given the opportunity to move, she didn't want to. The reason was because she was 'kind of' comfortable with her present job, even though she hated it.

At her current job, she knew all the people, and she knew how to run the systems with her eyes closed. She hated the job but was 'kind of' comfortable with it at the same time.

You don't want to go through your life being 'kind of' happy with the situation.

You want to find a job or a career that you love to do. Yes, I know it's easier said than done, but it's important to be on the lookout for new opportunities and take those opportunities when they come along.

How many of us in life complain about things and when we have an opportunity to do something about the situation we don't make the change? Sometimes there are situations which are more difficult than others to change, but if we want to change the situation, then we have to get up and move our life in a different direction!

The girl never took the new job opportunity and stayed unhappy. Or should I say, 'kind of' happy.

I asked her why she wouldn't take the new job opportunity. She said she didn't want to because she would have to meet new people and learn new systems there. And what if it turned out worse than the job she's got, she thought?

When you start something new, it's always challenging at first, but within a short time you will normally settle into it by the end of a month.

The reason the girl never took the job was because of fear, fear of the unknown, fear of what would happen if she took the new job. Instead of looking at the possibilities and how things could be much better, she thought about the negative aspects of the new job.

And what if she found she didn't like her new job, or what if her new boss fired her?

Then she would be in trouble with the payments of her car, her gas bill, her electric bill, her phone bill. She would fall back on the payments for that other loan she got out years before, and OH MY GOD... she might lose her house and have to beg on the street!

Besides, she had to travel on a new route to work. But she didn't know the route as well as her usual route. She could have an accident... Heck, she could even be killed!

I don't want to sound as if I don't care about that person because I do care, but people sometimes build mountains out of molehills and talk themselves out of a brilliant life!

Whether it's fear, lack of courage, or laziness, they are all things that will hold you back in life.

"So you need to man the fuck up, take the bull by the horns, and just go for it!"

Yes, there is risk in starting anything new, but if you don't stretch yourself, you'll always stay in the same place.

If you want to do well in this life, you have to be constantly learning. You have to put yourself into situations where you're meeting new people.

When I joined the army, there was a part of me that didn't want to leave home. But I felt that I was so useless back then and I wouldn't be able to get a good job at home. Yes, there was a lot of uncertainty, but I was willing to take the risk.

Were there aspects of the army that were shit? You bet there were! However, even though there were negative aspects of the armed forces, it also helped me with who I later became.

Taking a chance on going for the Commando Course and getting into 29 Commando was the most significant thing I had done until that point in my life.

The other, and far more significant thing that I did in my life was, read books and listen to audios on personal development.

Did some people think these books wouldn't help me and take the piss out of me for reading them? Yes! Were those piss taking people living the type of life that I wanted to live? No!

Did these books help me create the dream life that I enjoy today?

"Fuck yes!"

No matter how challenging things get for you and no matter what you go through, you can overcome it!

There is a better life out there waiting for you, and it's there for you to claim.

So man the fuck up, change what needs to be changed, and...

GO FOR IT!

ACKNOWLEDGEMENTS

It's almost impossible to say how many people have helped me along the way with producing this book, and if you're not in the acknowledgements just know that I am very grateful for your support and help.

However, I would like to say a massive THANK YOU to a few people that I can think of, off the top of my head:

Paul 'The Viking' Hughes, Tom Webb, Eva Savage, Mark 'Billy' Billingham, Julie Colombino-Billingham, Tracy, Kay and Maria Morris, Cheryl Hicks, Jamie Baulch, Gene Hipgrave, Tom Hughes, Kauri-Romet Aadamsoo, Mark Dawson, Craig Martelle, Michael Anderle, Michael and Emma Byrne, Paul 'Faz' Farrington, Paul Heaney, James Atkinson and Laura Taylor.

Also, a huge THANKS to 'The Mark Llewhellin Advance Reader Team' for taking the time to read the manuscript and make suggestions.

Live Your Dreams!

Mark

ABOUT THE AUTHOR

In 1990, Mark Llewhellin left school without knowing his grades. He had little confidence and was not at all optimistic about his future.

Not knowing what to do with his life Mark followed some of his friends into the Army. He failed his basic 1.5-mile run, was bullied, and was also voted the fattest person in the Troop!

After a year with the Junior Leaders Regiment Royal Artillery, Mark decided he would try and get into 29 Commando Regiment Royal Artillery, which is an elite Army Commando Regiment that at the time proudly held the Military Marathon World Record (i.e. a marathon carrying a 40lbs backpack).

After failing the 29 Commando Selection phase (called 'The Beat Up') twice, first through lack of fitness and secondly through an injury, Mark subsequently passed on his third attempt and completed the 'All Arms Commando Course' on his first attempt.

Mark later went on to achieve the following:

- Break the 100-kilometre Treadmill World Record.

- Place 1st in the Strava Distance Challenge in 2015 competing against over 51,000 runners.

- Place 1st in the Strava Distance Challenge in 2014 competing against over 40,000 runners.

- Run and walk 70-miles without training on his 40th birthday.

- Become a successful Personal Fitness Trainer.

- Complete the Marathon Des Sables (a six-day, 135-mile ultra-marathon in the Sahara Desert).

- Work and live in London's exclusive Park Lane as a Bodyguard.

- Run 1,620 miles in the United States whilst carrying a 35lbs pack.

Mark has interviewed some of the world's top performers and high achievers in various locations, including one of the world's most prestigious memorabilia rooms...the Hard Rock Café Vault Room in London.

He has travelled to over 50 countries and has been featured in leading national newspapers and on TV for his running achievements.

Mark has extensively worked in the support and care industry for many years helping individuals with brain injury, autism, epilepsy, dyspraxia, and various types of learning difficulties.

He is the Managing Director of Mark 7 Productions, as well as the Producer and Host of 'An Audience with Mark Billy Billingham' speaking events around the UK.

Mark is currently working on more personal development books and lives with his son Léon (when Léon's not at his Mum's) on a beautiful marina in South West Wales.

ALSO BY MARK LLEWHELLIN

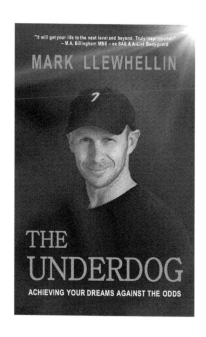

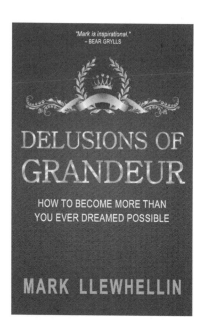

IF YOU ENJOYED THIS BOOK

Your help in spreading the word about Mark's books is greatly appreciated and your reviews make a huge difference to help new readers change their lives for the better.

If you found this book useful please leave a review on the platform you purchased it on.

MARK LLEWHELLIN BOOKS OUT IN 2020

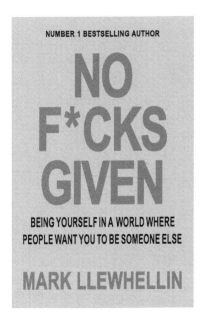

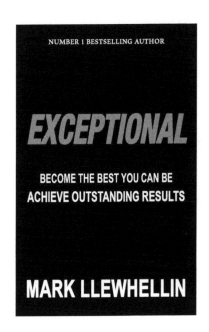

GET TWO FREE MARK LLEWHELLIN BOOKS AND DEALS AND UPDATES

Join 'The Mark Llewhellin Advance Reader Team' for information on new books and deals plus:

You can pick up FREE copies of Mark's five star reviewed books:

1. 'The Underdog'

2. 'Delusions of Grandeur'

Simply go to Mark's website at www.markllewhellin.com and sign up for FREE.

REFERENCES

The Tim Ferris Show

Left to Tell: One Woman's Story of Surviving the Rwandan Genocide By Immaculée Ilibagiza

Wikipedia

DISCLAIMER

Although the author and publisher have made every effort to ensure that the information contained in this book was accurate at the time of release, the author and publisher do not assume and hereby disclaim any liability to any party for any loss, damage, or disruption caused by errors or omissions in this book, whether such errors or omissions result from negligence, accident, or any other cause.

A Mark 7 Publications Paperback.

First published in Great Britain in 2020

by Mark 7 Publications

Copyright © Mark 7 Publications 2020

ISBN 978-1-914006-00-5

Book design and formatting by Tom Webb
pixelfiddler@hotmail.co.uk

Printed in Great Britain
by Amazon

51125206R00090